# Along



Prudence Jarrett

Very best wishes
Prudence M Jarrett

All scripture is from the King James Version
of the Holy Bible.

British Library Cataloguing In Publication Data
A Record of this Publication is available
from the British Library

ISBN 1846850401
978-1-84685-040-0

First Published February 2006 by

Exposure Publishing,
an imprint of Diggory Press,
Three Rivers, Minions, Liskeard, Cornwall, PL14 5LE, UK

WWW.DIGGORYPRESS.COM

# *Dedication*

This book is dedicated to all those who will read it and find the courage to move on in faith.

Acknowledgements

With special thanks:

To my colleagues and friends, Marianne Cook and Diane Hargreaves, for their encouragement, support and prayers.

To my husband, Dave, for his interest in my work.

To my son, David, for his love and understanding.

To Winsone Ruddock-Cole for your prayers.

To Pastor and Mrs Ferguson, and the members of the Free Presbyterian Church of London for your encouragement and prayers.

To my friends and acquaintances who have motivated me to share some of my experiences.

# *Contents*

# Along The Way

# *Introduction*

## *In His Presence*

IT IS amazing how the Holy Spirit inspires us when we come away with the Word of God. It does not matter how intellectual, wealthy, poor or wretched we feel or are; the Holy Spirit can teach, exhort, rebuke, reprove and lead us into all truth.

This book was born out of a meeting with Jesus one morning during my devotion. I was going through a very hard time and could hardly express how I felt to the Lord. It just felt like my prayers were being stopped and God was unreachable. I began to leaf through my Bible, stopping ever so often to read an underlined portion of Scripture that had meant a lot to me. As I leafed through, something wonderful began to happen to me. I began to thank God for the times when He came through for me. Along the way, God delivered me; along the way, God protected me; along the way, God manifested his love towards me and granted me special favours and along the way, He sacrificed His only Son, Jesus, just for me. The more I thought about the ups and downs along the way, the more the Holy Spirit impressed upon my mind the title for this book, *Along the Way*.

When I remembered God's goodness, I began to praise Him and I felt myself gradually enter into His presence. I told Him how much I loved and appreciated Him and I confessed my sins because it was my ingratitude, doubt and short-sightedness that had caused the separation. I then told the Lord my troubles and I told Him that I would trust His Word. Well, I can tell you, and make no mistake, my burdens rolled away. Not that the situation changed immediately, but I regained my focus and today, I am able to share with you some of the experiences I have garnered along the way, in the hope that they will encourage you to trust in the Living God.

# *Chapter 1*

## *Childhood Fantasies*

I GREW up in a large family and falling somewhere in the middle; I had a fair grasp of the ways of my older brother and sister, yet I could enter into the time and space of my younger siblings. Most certainly, I did not want to experience the wretchedness and misery of my older siblings, so I often meandered in my thoughts to better and more wonderful 'nobler' things, as a way of escape.

I had dreams about the way I wanted to live. I wanted parents who had lots of money or at least be financially comfortable. I would even imagine myself all dressed up in pretty frocks and riding in one of those fishtail cars, instead of riding on the bar of my father's prized bicycle, in a print dress, sometimes with no shoes on. My little mind saw pretty ribbons, dainty shoes and frilly socks and lots and lots of delicious food.

I wanted to live in a lovely big house that had a maid to do the washing up, cooking and cleaning, especially for mum, who had the hardest time keeping her tiny house in a hygienic condition. I wanted my own room, my space, and to be able to invite those I wish to enter at will, and keep out those (siblings) who would create a mess.

But, my ultimate childhood fantasy was to become someone important. I wanted to become a nurse. Foremost, I think, I wanted to become a nurse to take care of my mum, who continually suffered from (what I later learnt) peptic ulcers. Of course, I wanted to earn a lot of money and be able to do what I pleased with it.

Yes, then they were fantasies but today I look back and I think: Those were the thoughts that propelled me forward, but given a chance they could have destroyed me too. The mind is a powerful organ for it has the resilience to make us princes or paupers, believers or doubters. No wonder the Word of God makes it very clear that we should… 'gird up the loins of [our] mind, be sober, and hope to the end for the grace that is to be brought unto [us] for the revelation of Jesus Christ as obedient children...' (1 Peter 1:13 KJV) When we do this, God promises that He will exalt us as we follow Christ: 'And being found in fashion as a man, He humbled himself and became obedient unto death, even the death of the cross. Wherefore, God highly exalted Him and gave Him a name above every other name.' (Phil. 2: 8-9, KJV) It is very important to note that verses 8-9 depend on verse 5: 'Let this mind be in you, which was also in Christ Jesus…'

*What are you thinking about these days?*

# *Chapter 2*

# *A Feeling*

JUST recently, a friend and I were bemoaning the fate of elderly female pensioners who are being mugged for the few pennies that they have. The conversation began because my friend, who had her handbag safely tucked under her arm and held in a vice grip; saw me loosely holding mine as though I had nothing to lose. She warned: 'You had better hold on to your handbag, because youths are riding on their bikes, and grabbing ladies' handbags. It is not good enough to put it under your arm; you must hold on to it.' Well, I took her advice since she was able to cite, convincingly, the experiences that some of her friends had had.

For a few minutes the conversation lulled and I went into reflect mode. I thought about the time when I was walking in Kingston, Jamaica, amidst the hustle and bustle of the crowd, when all of a sudden I felt a kind of electric shock wave pass through my body. I thought for only a second that that was unusual then turned around only to see a man in his twenties reaching out to take my handbag. He was just as shocked as I was, so he turned and ran away.

Another time, I had gone into the Mandeville market to buy vegetables, but getting out was slow for there were higglers milling about with their wares and the shoppers found it necessary to stop every so often to pick up this and that. Just as I was about to exit the market, I felt a shockwave pass through me and I remembered what happened in Kingston. I turned around only to see a man reaching out with his penknife to cut my bag strap. He panicked and quickly disappeared when I turned around because he was hoping that I would think that it was an innocent fellow shopper who had rubbed against me.

I recounted these stories to my friend and she told me that the experiences were extraordinary.

I certainly cannot give an account for this unusual occurrence, but I believe that it resonates in the Bible, the very Word of God. The unusual occurrences might be different, for God uses various methods to protect His children, just as He uses different people with varying gifts, in this world, to be of help to their fellowmen. Not only that, God uses his angels and the Holy Spirit to guide us out of danger. It is a wonderful feeling and assurance to know that 'Because [we] have made the Lord, who is [our] refuge, even the Most High, [our] habitation...no evil shall befall [us]...for he shall give his angels charge over [us] to keep [us] in all our ways.' (Psalm 91: 9-11, KJV)

*One thing we can be sure of: we* ***cannot always*** *depend on our feelings, but we* ***can always*** *depend on God's Word!*

# Chapter 3
# A Hand

I HAD just left high school and was searching for a job as my father had made it very clear that after high school I had to 'paddle my own canoe.' I was terrified because my aspiration to go to college was dashed. Most of my peers were certain that they were going to be going to college in the autumn term. Nevertheless, I had still kept the dream alive that I wanted to become someone important, not in a selfish way, for I wanted to make my contribution to my family and country. I was still determined that somehow I would be the recipient of a college education.

Well, graduation came and I was decked out quite nicely because my mom impressed upon my father the need for me to be a part of the graduating class. I was thrilled, but that nagging feeling that I had reached a dead-end refused to leave me.

The summer months came and went and no one responded to my job applications. With nothing to do in September, I decided to go into Kingston to find work. Of course, I would stay with my grandmother and hopefully earn enough to pay for my board and keep. My mother really did not want me to go, but I convinced her that it was better to try than to sit down idly. So I went into Kingston. September passed; October passed; November came and there was no job.

I remembered thinking that I was not going to amount to anything and at times I would break down in tears. I refused to eat partly because I had lost my appetite, as is expected when you are fed once per day. I was as thin as a wafer.

It was one of those days when I was at my lowest that something marvellous happened to me. I was sitting on my bed, with my back turned to the door, sobbing, for I did not think that I could sink any lower. However, I became aware of a presence in the room and a hand on my shoulder. I stopped with a gasp out of embarrassment as I had thought that my grandmother had slipped into the room without my being aware. When I plucked up enough courage to look around, to my astonishment, no one was there. Suffice it to say: I cannot forget the healing touch of that Hand to this day!

It had to have been the Holy Spirit! Today, I remember and I rejoice, that the Great God of Heaven would come to me in my distress and bring healing. The story did not end there. I got up, showered, dressed myself and walked to the end of my road to enquire if the manager of a woodwork shop needed a worker. He interviewed me and the following Monday morning, I was heading to work. No wonder David, the Psalmist, exhorts us to 'Trust in [God] at all times; pour out your heart before Him you people. God is a refuge for us.' (Psalm 62:8, KJV)

*Remember: 'This poor man cried, and the Lord heard him, and saved him out of all his troubles.' (Psalm 34:6)*

# *Chapter 4*

# *Unspeakable Moments*

THERE are times when I think that God gets his kicks from doing the unusual, for he gets double applause for confounding and amazing us. This is one such occasion when He did just that.

I was working as a governess for a wealthy family in the USA and they were quite good to me initially, for I took care of their children. That allowed them time to play and do the things that they wanted, never mind the children. They had no conscience when it came to encroaching on my time-off. I was definitely not pleased and I did let them know that. The two children became very close to me because I mothered them day in, day out. I thought, at the time, that that was not healthy for the children and I had what amounted to a meeting, to explain my observations regarding the children's need. That incurred the wrath of their mom, for in fact they were paying me to do a job.

It was Christmas time, and anybody who knows about Christmas in America knows well that it is a big thing! In any case, the New Year was coming up and as a custom this family planned a huge and prestigious party where the richest and the best attended. It was a fairy tale event! Fortunately for me, the New Year fell on my day-off and I had planned for months that I would be attending the New Year's Eve Watch Night Service with my cousins. They thought going to church was a waste of time because, after all, there was no such person as God.

They had to work hard for their money and the things that they had. Nevertheless, I had made it clear that I would leave after their party had begun, since I thought they would need some assistance with getting the children ready. I thought that was fair, but they thought that I was selfish though I reminded them of the agreement.

I was very upset and very annoyed that I had to stay among people who thought that I should ask their permission to live. I discovered that I could seek some compassion from Mr. Vee* but not his wife, and after a discussion, he decided that I could go once the party got on the way. I was happy and helped to get things in order, not forgetting to park my car on the outside, so that I would not be backed in when it was time for me to leave. Of course, Mrs. Vee* was quite pleased with herself because she had thought I was caught out by that minor detail.

One of the things I had to do was guide the caterers who not only brought the cutlery, crockery, table cloths, but the flooring that would transform the tiled patio into that of a wooden, laminated ballroom floor. They did their job with great skill and I was quite pleased with the effect. Towards nightfall, the host got dressed in his tuxedo and went down to check that all things fell into place, while I got the children dressed. Mrs. Vee* would be the last to get dressed for she always liked to make an entrance.

Mr. Vee* noticed something quite out of the ordinary. The wooden floors began to spring water, so he asked one of the helpers to mop them, but the more they mopped, the more the water sprang up. It was as if a spring had been encased in the panels of the flooring boards. They called for the entire dozen extra large beach towels to soak up the water with very little result. Taps were checked; the patio covering was checked for any possible leaks; there were no signs of seepage and it was not raining.

There was nothing more that I could do, so I got dressed and without creating much attention, I wished them a good night and bade them goodbye.

Tuesday evening came and I returned to work, only to be told of the events of the New Year's Eve party. The revellers in their half drunk dancing state had totally forgotten the wet floor and in their heightened state of excitement began to slip, slide and tumble over each other. Some had broken wrists, ankles, fractured ribs, bruises and welts. Many of the guests had to be taken to the hospital. Mrs.Vee* suffered a broken wrist. I was in shock, to say the least, when I returned and saw my employer's wrist in a cast. The irony was that I should have deemed this poetic justice, but I was truly sorry about what had happened. I told Mrs. Vee* that I was truly sorry that she had broken her wrist. I got a sense that she feared that I would have rejoiced over her mishap, but I had disappointed her yet again.

All the fancy food was collected and put away in the huge refrigerators for use at a later date. Mrs. Vee told me that she had not had any of the food on the night of the party, as we sat to eat some of what was left over on the Wednesday following. Up to the time I left that employment, no one had been able to explain what happened that night. The caterers did return to check the floors and they were as dry as ever.

I can only say that this remarkable happening was an act of God for it defied explanation. Moreover, I believe that when these events occur in our lives we need to examine ourselves in the light of our relationship with God and our neighbour. We cannot read the account of Hezekiah and not understand the power of the Living God, and how He defends those who trust in Him. The blasphemous king, Sennacherib, for a considerable length of time intimidated Hezekiah, and threatened the very existence of the Jewish nation, but God would consider the prayers of one intimidated king. The result: 'The angel of the Lord went forth and smote in the camp of the Assyrians a hundred and eighty-five thousand; and when [Hezekiah's men] arose early in the morning, behold these were dead.' (Isa.37: 36) Moreover, Sennacherib returned to Assyria and while he was worshipping his idol, his own son assassinated him.

No wonder the Word of God charges us **not** to be wise in our own eyes, but to 'fear the Lord' and depart from evil, as 'it shall be health to [our] navel, and marrow to [our] bones.' (Proverbs 3: 7-8)

*Has God spoken to you today through an unusual circumstance? What did you hear Him say?*

* Not their real names

# *Chapter 5*

# *The Gift of Laughter*

I HAVE brothers and sisters who are endowed with the gift of humour. They only need to start telling a funny story or joke and you would laugh until you cry. I could not understand how one could be comical without a smidgen of a smile on the face, but my siblings can. Before I understood how blessed I was, I envied my brothers and sisters who could bring comic relief to just about anyone who would listen. I guess they got this from both our parents: a mother who could earn a living as a ventriloquist and a father who had drama and comedy embedded in his personality.

The thing is, if I have to give a joke, I always have to recount the story in my head and make up my mind that I am not going to laugh, thereby giving away the punch line; but the opposite always happens. I have had to concede that comedy is just not one of my many gifts.

However, I realised something quite remarkable about myself: I have the gift of laughter. I enjoy a good laugh and if you have a good joke, then you do not have to look very far for an audience; it is right there in me. So my brothers and sisters love to be around me for they like telling jokes because they know that I like to laugh. What a wonderful combination! I now look back and castigate myself for being so foolish when I was specially gifted, myself. I think also that the spin-off of this gift is an optimistic spirit which says 'I can do; I can be.'

When I began teaching abroad, I remembered going home after the first day to share the antics of the children with my flatmates, for if I did not do that I would have wept and become depressed. Then I was glad that I could laugh. We shared and laughed until the tears rained down our cheeks and what a relief we felt! We were refreshed and we slept very well, and you would not believe that we had gone through such a harrowing day and were looking forward to the next. We were practically living out Proverbs 17: 22 which declares 'A merry heart doeth good like a medicine…' for certainly 'a merry heart makes a cheerful countenance...' (Proverbs. 15:13)

Science is just now catching up to the Bible because doctors are now encouraging their patients to laugh more, for laughter medicates the soul. Do you want a bellyful of laughter? Then, read the Bible! What is more surprisingly hilarious than a donkey giving instructions to a man?

The God of wisdom has given us the wonderful gift of laughter. Let us use it to stave off some of the stresses and strains of life.

# *Chapter 6*

## *Trust*

I AM often quite a practical person who likes certainty and order. I tend to jump ahead of myself at times because I need to know that things will work tomorrow, to the extent that I sometimes do not enjoy today. I believe this is what they call worry and fear. Even as a child I felt that if I did not do some aspect of the household chores, it would not be properly done. Certainly, I was a hard worker, but I feared that my parents would not see that, and no rewards would come to me (selfishness).

My fear was very evident around Christmas time, perhaps because I was born around that time. I feared that my parents would not be able to give me that special gift that I had spoken about liking; not directly telling them to purchase it, but 'a wink to an old horse is just as good as a nod'; so as a child you would expect them to take the hint. A few times they took the hint, but at other times they just did what they wanted to. I learnt early that my parents were never going to pander to my wants and fears; they wanted me to trust them and develop the attitude of gratitude.

I can remember worrying one Christmas whether I was going to get a new dress when I was about fifteen years old. My parents had gone out shopping early Christmas Eve morning and I was left at home to make sure the cleaning was done. Now that I think about it, I was angry and the anger propelled me along like a steam locomotive just because I could not comfort my heart that my parents would remember to bring me that outfit that I had wanted. Time creeps when you are angrily waiting for it. And anger boils when you are also 'ignored' for your anger is easily read on the face. The suspense is killing and you want to say, 'Hurry and show me what you have got for me!' But you can't; you have to wait. They not only brought me back a dress much better than the one I had wanted, they had the shoes and handbag to go with it. Needless to say, I felt so ashamed.

I have been embarrassed quite a few times because I simply would not take

God at His Word. I am certainly a work in progress and I am learning to heed His command: 'Trust in the Lord with all your heart and lean not unto your own understanding. In all your ways acknowledge him and He will direct your path.' (Proverbs 3:5-6) 'Oh, taste and see that the Lord is good; blessed is the man who puts his trust in Him.' God is a Promise-Keeper '…for there is no lack to them that fear Him. (Psalm 34:8-9) God is faithful and he rewards those who put their trust in Him.

You see, if my earthly parents could give me so much thought and attention beyond my expectation, what about my Heavenly Father?

*My Heavenly Father cares for me.*

# *Chapter 7*

## *Protection*

I WAS in deep thought some time ago about the way in which my life has gone. For some reason, I have always felt like I have been safeguarded throughout my entire life. I thought about my position in my family. My older siblings protected me from the strains attendant with older siblings and I got a fighting chance to get an education and a fairly decent life. Then I began to think about other people who nurtured and validated me by simply treating me with respect and care.

One day, just as my friends and I were going to exit the town in which our little primary school was situated, a heavy downpour--more like a storm--stopped us under a piazza, before a haberdashery store. It rained and rained as if it would not stop. It was well after 5:30 and the rain persisted. We were drenched, shivering from the cold, hungry and a long way from home. I was only a seven-year old finger-sucking gal. I looked inside and I longed to be in a dry and warm place. As if the proprietress read my mind, she came out on the piazza and began to have a conversation with us. We were thrilled! She invited us in; cleaned us; put dried clothes on us and fed us. They then drove us to the nearest points to our homes. I look back and I bless those good old days when people cared and were not afraid to show it.

I reflected on a friend, whom I had to abandon during my early teenage years, not because I could explain the uneasiness that came over me especially when she wanted to go across the neighbouring high school to meet up with 'friends'. I remember reasoning with myself about how wrong it was for me to be in uniform walking home with a boy. Plus I knew that it was nothing for my parents to give me a whipping for showing up after hours. Without anybody saying anything to me, I dropped my friend's company. Before long my ex-friend dropped out of school and later I learned, she became a prostitute. But for God's grace and mercy, I could have gone down that route! Thank God, I was protected!

I now look back and I can say for sure that my becoming a Christian as a teenager saw me through rough patches.

I had friends who were God-fearing and very protective of me. I went to places where I could meet young people who held similar beliefs as I and I was happy--in fact very happy!

I think of being in the safety of a Christian college and the respect and high expectations accorded me. I think of being housed on the campus of the university, just across from the library that made life a bit easy since I did not have to fear attacks because of distance. I think of being housed in a safe dormitory with girls who had the same values as I.

I could write a book replete with times when I felt very protected from terrible situations in my life. I realise that God was at work at every turn and created significant moments that have made me what I am today. I still enjoy God's protection and I lean heavily on Him for He is able and that is why I am able to say: 'The Lord is my rock, and my fortress, and my deliverer; my God, my strength, in whom I will trust; my shield and the horn of my salvation, and my high tower.'(Psalm 18:2)

*'The eye of the Lord is upon those who fear Him.' (Psalm 33:18)*

# *Chapter 8*

## *Trials*

I FIND that my greatest trials come just after I have had some victory or success for this is when I am lulled into a false sense of personal security. On the other hand, I find that as I go through, there is a lesson for me to learn that usually humbles me and causes me to rise to the next level.

After I left the university and returned to my substantive job, I least expected to experience what was to be a very significant drop in my personal morale. I had just gained extra knowledge and I had had so much to share but there was not that special opening that could accommodate me and I felt locked in and frustrated. I decided to go for a position that would enable me to work with my colleagues, but that position was taking far too long to come to fruition, as the government could not decide on its funding. In the mean time, another opening loomed and it was the agreement that I would fill that position. That was not to be because my head said that I could not go for both positions simultaneously, which I thought was unfair. You see, I am a believer in 'first come, first serve'; therefore when it's my turn you had better not step in my way. I felt it was my turn since I had allowed others to go ahead of me! I made it very clear and I went to all lengths to make it known. Well, I got neither position though I staked my claim as vociferously as I could orally and in writing. I was denied. There was no compromising with me, for I felt that I was unfairly treated.

The overwhelming thing is that I was not only experiencing a hard time at work, I was under the strain of a marriage that was in ruins for my husband and I could not see eye-to-eye on many issues and this was tearing us apart. It was one massive headache. Our son was going through a rebellious phase and our coping skills were frayed to say the least. It just seemed like all hell broke loose and I could not handle it!

I coped by repeating the injustices, and making what amounts to enemies for those who were making my life a misery, and the more I did that the more miserable I became. I had lost sight of God's purpose in all of this. Well, for one year I was only required to do my job, without extra responsibilities and I felt like I was being punished and sidelined. But, one day I received a telephone call from the University asking me to carry out a research on a particular topic in reading. I was pretty taken as I was being considered to write for an educational journal! This meant validation and new perspective! For the next several months, I was engrossed in research and I was very happy. I can safely tell you now that if I had had that extra position that I was gunning for, I could not have taken up that offer.

It was during that time that I began to reflect and introspect and I realised that I needed to learn forgiveness and patience with people and to always trust God for his provisions. Now I look back and I can say that that year was a most progressive and rewarding one, but I could have lost it all by demanding my own way.

The following year, without my even desiring a supervisory position (for my focus was on bigger and better things) I was forced to take up the very position that I had desired hitherto. Things calmed down on the home front and I was able to make peace with those I had offended. I did not then feel that I was entitled one way or the other.

In the first Epistle of Peter there is a solemn, but encouraging reminder: 'Beloved, think it not strange concerning the fiery trial which is to [test] you, as though some strange thing happened unto you, but rejoice…'(1Peter 4:12-13b) And, the Psalmist, David, underscores how temporary trials are when he says;

'Weeping may endure for a night, but joy cometh in the morning.' Therefore when I find that I am going through a rough patch, I draw heavily upon God's Word because I know that I am going through a period of transition that will affect my life positively. Any athlete will tell you that it is in the pain and daily grind of flexed muscles that they become victors at the end of a race.

*Think back on some of your trials to see how far along you have come!*

## *Chapter 9*

# *Providence*

WE CANNOT escape the fact that we live in a disposable world, for the media, (driven by politics, technology and economics), do not give the slightest reprieve; it is in your face. So we have disposable plates, cups, knives… disposable cameras, disposable incomes, disposable wives and husbands… disposable parents, and now a disposable God! Amazing!

The pace is fast and cut-throat because it is a harsh world out there: the books have got to balance; the quick buck will have to be made; the wheeling and dealing will have to be done between a power lunch and signing on the dotted line; the family will just have to learn how to get on with it if they want the luxuries and the money to acquire more luxuries; and to make it, less than 16 hours a day will not do and it goes on and on…

The flip side to this is a driven society that is tired, weary and worn. Even with double salaries, some just eek out a living and some fall into all kinds of monetary traps. Some get mixed up in the wrong crowd and even lose their reputation and lives, while others lose husbands and wives, never mind the children, for if one is to survive one has to put in the hours. Then there is the lament that children are unruly, selfish and in need of good manners.

I remember when I was growing up how fulfilled I felt just returning from school and seeing my mother at home. She did not have much by way of money; it was cutting and carving, planting a backyard garden; painstakingly patching and mending our clothes, but after that we were clean and covered; and trusting God to provide at every point and He did not disappoint. She raised us as part of a community, therefore we learnt respect early, and that community took their responsibility seriously for theirs was the responsibility to guide us. And, there was nothing disposable about it! Fast food was not a substitute for a home-cooked, sit-down-meal- with- the- family.

Today, 'community' has been lost as each person looks about himself. There is little or no dependence upon God, the

Creator; no quiet time spent in His Presence; and no Sabbath rest from the daily grind. We are a stressed-out, fast-food orientated-society that has become candidates for every kind of disease known to man.

I believe that we can get back to that place where we engage our clocks, beginning with the acknowledgment of God. Perhaps if we start off with a healthy concept about God, all the little bits will fall into place. His Word says: 'The blessing of the Lord makes rich, and he adds no sorrow with it.' (Proverbs 10:22) It is never God's intention to allow us to be poor and sick, in fact, He said to the Children of Israel, lest they said that it was their hard work that had got them their wealth: 'But thou shall remember the Lord thy God; for it is He who gives you power to get wealth, that he may establish his covenant which he swore unto your fathers…' (Deut. 8:18)

***Remember:***

*'No good thing will [God] with-hold from them that walk uprightly' (Ps. 84:11b) for He is Jehovah-jireh, your Provider.*

# Chapter 10

# Diligence

THERE is something to be said for the person who diligently does what he has to do, regardless of the circumstances or the context. I have always admired the student or the individual who is a plodder; he just hangs in there like a dog with a bone. I had a friend like that!

My friend taught me in her unique way how to take tiny steps until a goal has been reached. Amy* was not the brightest student in the class, but she was one of the most confident. She was careful about the neatness of her uniform; every pleat had to be in place; she neatly held

---

* Not her real name

them down then she sat. Amy* had to be at school rain or shine, for she could not afford to miss any of the lessons. School was important for her since she was the first in the family to enter high school and she took it seriously. Amy had to understand what the lesson was about and though it took sometime to clarify ideas, she would not have it any other way. She made neat notes and she asked lots of questions. Sometimes the members of the class were happy that Amy had asked a particular question as they had wanted to, but were shy or too proud to admit that they did not understand.

I remember how Amy always insisted that I study with her when I would rather be chatting with my other friends. Reluctantly I was forced to revise after a staunch reminder that we would be getting that test or exam. You see, I always prided myself on only needing to read over the notes just before the exam, as labouring over notes was a boring exercise. I learnt the hard way that Amy was right; she always did well in her tests and exams, even better that those students who were academically astute.

I learnt that continual drops of water form a stream. In other words, if I need to keep my house clean, I must consistently carry out a system of maintenance on a daily basis; not only would my house be clean, but my job of cleaning would also be made easier.

The Bible is replete with examples of the benefits of being diligent. 'He becomes poor that deals with a slack hand, but the hand of the diligent makes rich. He that gathers in the summer is a wise son, but he that sleeps in harvest is a son that causes shame. ' (Proverbs 10:4-5)

Many of the Parables of Jesus have to do with being diligent, for Jesus wanted his hearers to see the value - links, such as honesty, trustworthiness, patience; being able to manage and use one's creative imagination. The parables almost always end with the unfruitful, indulgent servant being deprived of some blessing or other and given a severe punishment. But the diligent, industrious servant is amply rewarded and promoted. This resonates in Proverbs 22:29 'Seest thou a man diligent in his business? He shall stand before kings; he shall not stand before mean men.'

*Have you started a project lately, but can't be bothered to complete it? There are always lessons to be learnt when we are diligent—FAITH and GOOD SUCCESS.*

# *Chapter 11*

## *Partnership*

LATELY, I have been thinking about the importance of partnerships. Some business entrepreneurs will say that partners have strengthened their businesses and others will say that partners have ripped them off. However, when I was growing up the old Jamaican proverb 'two coco-heads are better than one' always proved true when a difficult decision had to be made. Partnerships almost always give some emotional and mental reassurance to those who seek them. This is very true in the partnerships that little children forge.

I remember playing 'dolly house' when I was a little girl with my brothers and sisters. This mimicked our real home for there was a mother, a father, and children. Mother would do the housework and look after the doll, a cho-cho [fruit] with sticks stuck in for arms and legs, and the dad was expected to go out and do the work and bring in the money (flat stones). The 'dad' was also expected to build the house, which was made from pieces of sticks and banana leaves. The wonderful thing about this was that the 'mom' and 'dad' had to make the decisions and what they decided on, happened. In a roundabout way, we were developing our negotiating skills and social partnerships.

I see children working in partnerships in play and they invariably work out their problems with adult-like precision. It is interesting to see even an individual child playing by himself speak openly to himself as he makes decisions about what he is doing as if he were speaking to a partner.

As I read the Bible I cannot help but see the whole idea of partnership woven in every event in the Holy Script. In the Creation Story recorded in Genesis, "God said, Let us make man in our image, after our likeness; and let them have dominion...' (Genesis 1:26) The reader gets the impression that God is not speaking to himself, but to someone who is co-equal with Himself, such as Jesus or the Holy Spirit. Our wonderful Lord has shared Himself with human kind and has delegated some of his creative skills to us. As partners, we are to manage and take care of God's business on earth in the best possible way we know how. We are to exercise our power of choice to create good and forsake evil and the rewards will naturally flow to us.

Similarly, every time Jesus came upon a situation where he had to perform a miracle, he questioned the receiver, making sure that he created a partnership of faith. I think of the woman with the issue of blood. Jesus asked 'Who touched me?' (Luke 8:45) in the middle of a crowd, to the utter consternation of his disciples, then Jesus engaged her for she was a woman of faith: '...thy faith has made you well...' (Luke 8:48) When we believe in Jesus he does wonderful things through us.

Lastly, God sent His Son, Jesus Christ to partner with us in a personal way: 'For

God so loved the world that he gave his only begotten son, that whosoever believes on him should not perish but have everlasting life.' (John 3:16) Jesus took our sins and gave the currency of eternal life—full justification—and all we have to do is receive this marvellous gift.

Why not partner with Jesus today? He will give you joy unspeakable; a peace that passes all understanding and you can be sure that you have a divine representative in Heaven.

# *Chapter 12*

## *Favour*

WHEN I was growing up I was not one of the most attractive little girls you might meet in our little district. Why the other children called me 'Big Head' always puzzled me, for every time I looked in the hand-mirror, my head looked the right size. After a while, I thought, even as a child, that if that was how they saw my head then there was nothing that I could do about that! Plus my mother could only have us girls decked out during the holidays. Those were special times as we looked our prettiest and we became the talk of the district well after the holidays. I cannot remember receiving any special favours because I was who I was. Quite frankly, it did not bother me much, for one does not miss what one is not accustomed to.

Looking back through my child's eye, I did feel badly one time in particular when I was overlooked at a parish church treat for children. I, along with my brothers and sisters, had been invited to attend the Christmas Treat for children all around our little town. We were excited because our mother had told us some of what we could expect to do, see, and have. It promised to be an exciting time and we could not wait for the day to come.

In our Sunday best, we walked two miles to the parish church and by the time we got there it was teeming with children of all ages. The music, the decorations, the Christmas tree and good old Santa Claus grabbed our attention. Before long we had queued up to enter a very festive room. We went in orderly and took our places and for what seemed like forever the programme began with the singing of my favourite Christmas carols followed by the nativity. Then came Santa Claus with his bags of presents and every little boy and girl looked with great anticipation. The atmosphere was charged with excitement. Different ones went up for their presents, especially if they had finished eating their ice cream, and I went up, but for some strange reason, the man directing sent a few of us back to our seats. The others sneaked up and got theirs but I didn't.

I waited for him to call me to receive mine but he did not. I was too ashamed and shy to make a fuss about not getting a present, but I did feel badly, though it is only a faint memory now.

Being specially considered or given a favour usually refreshes the spirit and causes the receiver to have hope. This is played out as Jehovah, the 'I AM', commissions Moses to go down to Egypt to speak with king Pharaoh concerning freeing the Israelites from slavery. The message to the people was that God would give them favour in the sight of the Egyptians and that when they left Egypt they would not leave empty-handed. (Exodus 3:21 paraphrase) Did God keep His promise? Yes, He did! Later we see that 'the Lord gave the people favour in the sight of the Egyptians…' (Exodus 11:3) Further, 'And the Lord gave the people favour in the sight of the Egyptians, so that they gave unto them (the Israelites) such things as they required...' (Exodus 12:36) You see, the Egyptians collected gold, silver, clothing, cattle and camels and presented them as gifts to the Israelites.

Favour is over and beyond the blessings that we receive: it is divine overflow as Psalm 5:12 captures it: 'For You, Lord, wilt bless the righteous; with **favour** wilt thou compass him as with a shield.'

I am so very glad that no one can take away God's divine favour from me. I will never be overlooked in God's scheme of things (unless I walk away from Him) and no one is more important than I. I did not earn this favour; I simply accepted what Jesus did for me on the

Cross of Calvary: He took my sins upon himself and has set me free. Christ is now my mediator, advocate and intercessor in heaven and, in this world He has commissioned His Holy Spirit to teach, guard, reprove, exhort, comfort, protect and, to help me pray effectively.

*Pray that God will pour out His divine favour on you.*

# *Chapter 13*

## *Forgiveness*

THERE was a time when I could not understand the meaning of the word forgiveness, even though I was a practising Christian for years. This lack of understanding of the virtues of forgiveness began in the early years of my life. I did not particularly like my father who had very strict, mean and unyielding ways. As far as I was concerned, as soon as I could get out of his house, the better I would be. True to my word I finished college and took a job a long way from home, only managing to visit once a month.

Well I met my husband and he found out how I felt about my father and he encouraged me to forgive him because I could not hold a grudge since I was a born again Christian. Even though he made a lot of sense in my head, my heart always managed to rationalise my hurt, and the more I rationalised my hurt, the more I hurt. It was a cycle.

The strangest thing, however, was that I was not disrespectful to my father. A matter-of-fact, we used to have conversations, though I sensed that he would have liked for us to have longer ones. I also knew that he was actually proud of my achievements.

I learnt the hard way in marriage that it is a dangerous thing to carry a grudge against your spouse because it will invariably spill over and scorch the very ones that you love. For the record, I did not mean for it to hurt my family, but my tolerance for my husband's shortcomings was very low. The more I spoke out against them, the more bitter and disappointed I became; the more my husband made mistakes the more I resented him, and the cycle continued. I was always very ill in my stomach and though I went to the doctors, they still could not give a clear explanation for this discomfort. Much later, I learnt that I had had a hiatus hernia and that in order to keep well I had to be calm and eat properly (meaning bland and small amounts of food). There was the likelihood that this condition could get worse if I did not take care immediately.

I ran to the Lord Jesus Christ because I was in trouble! I told him all my troubles and I asked Him to forgive me. Things did not change, but my attitude towards those irritating habits and attitudes had begun to change. Incrementally, I was learning to forgive and my healing followed and today, I can safely say that I am a happier, healthier person for having forgiven my father and my husband.

I am so glad that God in His Wisdom has given us His Word as a blue print in this life in order for us to manage our health, finance, and relationship with Himself and our fellowmen. Jesus, after instructing His disciples how to pray, emphasised the need to forgive men their trespasses: 'For if you forgive men their trespasses, your heavenly Father will also forgive you; but if you forgive not men their trespasses, neither will your Father forgive your trespasses.' (Matthew 6:14-15) O, sometimes I struggle to forgive because the flesh likes to get its own way, but when I forgive quickly, I feel free from the heaviness that accompanies unforgiveness. I am able to move to the next level and I am able to gain new perspectives because I am walking in obedience to the Word and Will of God.

How do you know that you have forgiven someone? You can remember without that bitter retching in your stomach; you can walk on the same side of the road; you can reach out in love to give a helping hand and, you do not feel the need to share the fault with any one.

# *Chapter 14*

## *Singing*

I HAVE got to say that what passes for singing and music today is sometimes laughable. Then again, I will myself not to laugh because I remember a time when my mother used to get very annoyed because I was an 'ardent singer' and I just would not shut up. My mother thought that I was hopeless at singing and the more she wanted me to shut up, the more I sang. I now believe that she felt exactly how I feel about some of the singing that goes on now a days. Well, as a child I felt very badly and I believe that somewhere along the way, I kind of gave up (at least in public) as I could not hit the right notes, but privately I sang to my heart's content.

I remember visiting friends in Philadelphia whose middle child had a penchant for singing and acting and she made you know that by her continual dissonant performance. She was only 7 or 8 years old and many a time I had wanted to say 'Why don't you think of doing something else that you can safely manage?' But, I remembered how negative comments caused me to lose some of my confidence in singing. Bless her heart. I have not seen or heard from her in a very long time, but I hope that she is still singing.

I can safely tell you that one day this 'crow' turned out to be a melodious 'nightingale', for my mother and siblings got the chance to listen to me sing, in public for the first time and they were absolutely speechless. My private practice had paid off and I could indeed turn a tune. What a victory that was!

Singing does something very special to my heart. There is that sense of peace, contentment and lift that I feel, especially after a miserable day at work. I often forget my housework in the middle of doing it because singing takes the hassle and worry out of it. Sometimes, I forget that my son's socks and shoes are in the wrong place, or that the toothpaste is squeezed from the top down, instead of bottom up or that a plate is under the bed; all because I am caught up in singing.

In the light of my experience, I can understand why David, the Psalmist exhorts us to sing unto the Lord. He was a king who had seen troubles in his time. Think of king Saul who wanted him dead or alive; think of the envy and jealousy of his kinsmen; think of his family, separated by adultery, incest, murder and death. I believe that when David found himself in his various situations, he played his harp and sang to the Lord. It is out of his experience that he shouts across the annals of time: 'Make a joyful noise unto the Lord, all ye lands. Serve the Lord with gladness; come before His presence with singing.' (Psalm 100:1-2) And, declares: 'I will sing unto the Lord as long as I live; I will sing praise to my God while I have my being.' (Psalm 104:33)

*I have come to realise that there is healing to be had when we approach the Lord of Heaven with a song of praise.*

# *Chapter 15*

# *Giving*

I HAVE met people along the way who have been blessed with the gift of giving. I have often been inspired by their generosity and have often tried to pattern them. It just seemed that the more they gave, the more they had to give.

My aunt was a prime example of a very giving person. How well I remember my aunt today. She was not comfortably well off by any means. In fact, she and her husband were low-income workers, but one could hardly tell, for they never seemed to be in need. Of course, they were rich from my childish perspective! The wonderful thing about my aunt was that she was always giving. She always made sure that we got all kinds of goodies and pocket money and, did we feel special! When my aunt immigrated to the United States, she made it her point of duty to send a package or a barrel every holiday and she never failed to send the prettiest little dresses and the daintiest pairs of shoes for us girls and she always marked mine so there would be no confusion as to what belonged to whom. I believe that secretly my aunt 'adopted' me, for she tried her best to give me a little bit more than the others. Certainly, I did not realise that then, for which I am glad!

Similarly, I think of a friend of mine who inspires me with her giving. She committed herself to dress the Church with cut flowers every Sunday and what a blessing when we step into our place of worship! There they are: bouquets designed by a pair of well-trained hands, never mind the heart of a loving soul. Even when certain flowers are scarce, she seems to be able to ferret and present them with such ease. Even when they are costing an arm and a leg, she does not complain; she just keeps her personal commitment to the task. Bless her heart!

I think of a dear sister, also, who has now gone on to be with the Lord. Sister Collins knew exactly when to send a basket of goodies to our home, with all the items of food that we were in need of but could not afford to buy at that particular time. Not only that, she would put a few dollars in one corner of the bag, because she had been instructed to do so. The wonderful thing about Sister Collins was that the right hand did not know what the left hand did, since for her this was a ministry!

I must confess that deep down I want to give and I have often given and this has brought joy to my heart. On the other hand, I sometimes do not give because I begin to assess, even criticise, the thoughts and reactions of the receiver long before I have the gift. Then, on the basis of my conclusion, I give or do not give. O, but I have learnt something about giving! Giving is a decision we make; it is not a feeling, for feelings come and go! Giving benefits both the giver and the receiver. It is God's Law and it works every time.

The entire Bible embraces a culture of giving. Abraham gave 'tithe (one-tenth) of all' (Gen. 14:20) his possession to

Melchizedek, the high priest, in appreciation for the mighty victory that God had given him. Similarly, atonement and peace were given to those who gave their unblemished lambs, calves, rams, and bulls, first as an act of obedience to Jehovah, and second, to have the glory of the Lord in their presence. You see, the Law of Giving works every time: 'freely you have received; freely give' (Matthew 10:8) and this follows a cycle. If you withhold, the cycle is broken and neither the potential giver nor receiver benefits from the partnership, hence Jesus' admonition: 'It is more blessed to give than to receive.' (Acts 20:35)

Moreover, giving shows a deep understanding of the all-knowing God in whom we put our trust. Solomon, the playboy king, had a good grasp of this fact. He linked 'giving' with wisdom, as God's people are counted wise if they honour the Lord with their substance, and with the first fruits of all their increase; in order that their barns will be filled with plenty and their presses burst out with new wine (Proverbs 3:9, paraphrased). Here is a classic case of wisdom in action. Abigail averted war and murder when she brought foodstuff to David to assuage his fierce anger against her husband, Nabal. It was not long after that Nabal died and Abigail became King David's wife.

Most significantly, Jehovah gave His only Son, Jesus to die in our place on a cruel cross for a world crippled by sin. He knew that some would scourge, spit at and despise His special Gift, but He sent Jesus anyway. Now Jesus has declared

Himself: '...whosoever believeth in [the son of Man] should not perish, but have eternal life' (John 3:15).

A Wise God has given every human being the gift of giving. The wonderful thing is, the more you exercise the gift, the more capacity you create for giving because you will always have excess.

*Do not know if you have anything to give? Start clearing out your cupboards; start praying for your neighbours; start giving to your church or a charity; visit the elderly with a cooked meal; offer to do some maintenance work for the retired couple down the road…*

# *Chapter 16*

# *Surrender*

IT is true that self-preservation is the keenest sense that all living things have in common. Man is especially keen to preserve himself by fair or foul means; hence, it is nothing for him to annihilate millions just to safeguard his territory, which may be a religious, social or geographical one. In order to further preserve himself he will surrender to his enemies only to make sure that he stays alive.

The lower animal kingdom is no different. The fittest creatures or animals in the jungle will survive because they prey on those, which are weak and vulnerable. Yet given the chance to use their survival instincts, the vulnerable creatures always try to make a quick get-a-way, but always find that their puny efforts are no match for their mighty preys.

Sometimes I feel like those creatures that put up a fight for survival because I think that I have the ability to do so successfully, only to fall flat on my face. Sometimes I seem to win and I walk away with a head full of inflated pride, then realise that I am overtaken by some monstrous task, which knocks me back into the reality of submission. Sometimes it's an advice that I refuse to take and must concede to the silence of 'I told you so'.

It is never easy to surrender, but it is a safe place to be, because surrender brings some level of submission, empathy, love and mercy. Surrender makes one dependent on another or creates interdependence among groups and individuals, thereby creating social harmony.

Man's greatest enemy is the devil. He does not mind at all that nations are fighting against nations; children are disobedient to parents; governments have taken over the job of parents; prayer has been taken out of school; the Bible is ridiculed and disregarded; and that marriages are breaking apart. The Bible says that he goes around like a roaring lion, seeking whom he may devour (1 Peter 5:8); yet he has the power to be 'transformed into an angel of light' (2 Corinthians 11:14), giving a false sense of security because he is the father of lies

(John 8:44). And, he preys on our weaknesses and inadequacies and he even dares to point an accusing finger right in our faces. But our Mighty Conqueror, the Lord Jesus Christ defeated Satan on the Cross of Calvary when he took our sins upon Himself. Jesus' Blood has given us dual coverage: (1) it saves us from the wrath of God, because Jehovah is a holy God and cannot abide sin; and (2) it testifies against Satan that we are sealed unto Christ for always and Satan has no more power over us. All we have to do is surrender to the Will of God and take on the imputed righteousness of Jesus Christ. How do we do this? We confess our sins. We repent and ask God to forgive us and turn away from sinful practices. We openly show in water baptism that we are serious about our commitment to follow Jesus.

How do you maintain your faith in the Lord Jesus Christ? You seek the Lord in prayer. Continual prayer brings peace and it clarifies issues in our lives. Prayerfully read the Word of God, the Bible. Tell others about the love of Jesus and find a Bible-believing Church in which to worship your Heavenly Father and find fellowship with other believers.

*Look Out for Prudence Jarrett's*

*Next Book:-*

## *'A Leap'*

A LEAP... explores the life and times of a Jamaican family through its central characters, Phil and Robby. It is love at first sight, and not long after, marriage, but soon they would discover that they are from two different worlds that rarely ever meet. With the arrival of their children and the attendant ups and downs, twists and turns, hope almost dies. Almost – for they must hold on to that last thread of hope and take that leap...

Printed in the United Kingdom
by Lightning Source UK Ltd.
109943UKS00001B/136-519

9 781846 850400